Colour
Confidence

Colour Confidence

A Practical Handbook to Embracing Colour in Your Home

Jessica Sowerby

Photography by Anna Batchelor

Hardie Grant

QUADRILLE

For my darling Rick,

and for Donna, the colourful
soul who made him the
wonderful man he is.

INTRODUCTION

'What I need most of all is colour, always, always.'
Claude Monet, artist

Everyone is good at something. Some people excel at languages or shine at the sciences. I have a friend who is so skilled at biscuit eating, she can finish a whole packet of Jaffa Cakes in under three minutes. In my case, I have always been good at colour. I know that may seem a peculiar thing to say as colour isn't technically a tangible skill or activity, but it's something I've always had a knack for. There are loads of things I'm completely useless at, like sticking to a recipe or anything to do with numbers, but colour has always been my comfort zone, *my happy place*.

According to my mum, even as a very young child I would refuse to wear the practical outfits she picked out for me, instead choosing my own jazzy technicolour ensembles. Not content with just rainbow bedding and curtains, I insisted on lime-green walls and a sunshine-yellow ceiling – much to the dismay of my neutral-loving mum. Her idea of brightly coloured is throwing a blue into the otherwise safe mix.

People often say I am 'brave' for my use of colour, which I find a delightfully charming yet strange term. I'm not sleeping in a haunted house or holding a spider – truly courageous behaviour in my eyes.

Over the years I have come to realize that so many people who love colour are scared of using it in their homes. Some find it hard to pick a harmonious palette in the sea of colour cards; others are unable to visualize how a new scheme will look in their rooms. Such things hold them back from embracing the colours they love and makes them settle for something bland and, in their words, 'easy'. The thought of this upsets me.

For me, colour is happiness; it is how I express myself.

Some people say they would love to champion colour but are afraid to take the plunge. But if you think about it, colour is everywhere and in everything – once you learn to not only live with it, but embrace it with both arms, *that is when the true magic happens*.

Now, I don't want to get on my soapbox here, but I believe that your home should be an honest reflection of you and an inviting insight into your personality. My home is a peek behind the curtain into my mind – colourful and slightly cluttered with interior detritus, intriguing memories and character.

If you surround yourself with the colours that reflect who you are and what you love, coming home every day will be a joy.

Everyone has their own concept of what they consider colourful. This book isn't aiming to convince you to adorn your homes with flamboyant rainbows (unless that's your jam, of course). Instead, it aims to help you find your happy place when it comes to colour – whether that's a home of decadent jewel tones or a cosy warm neutral palette – and give you the courage to master it. It's time for some **colour confidence**.

01

FALL IN LOVE
WITH COLOUR

'Colour is a power which directly influences the soul.'
Wassily Kandinsky, artist

Let's paint a picture. It's a balmy summer evening; the vast expanse of sky is a soft denim shade, faded to cornflower, and scattered with cotton wisps of altocumulus clouds. Hazy bands of amber and blush glow from the horizon, turning your view into a masterpiece of colour gradients. Truly a work of art.

Nothing exhibits the wonder of colour better than nature. It is an endless, inexhaustible source of inspiration. The way a perfect sunset makes you feel is the mood I want to bring into my home and surround myself with. If you want your home to fill you with joy every time you walk through the door, **you first need to fall in love with colour**.

THE POWER COLOUR HOLDS

I have always considered colour integral to my life – not an afterthought but a real essential. In my early twenties I one day decided to rid my wardrobe of the last dregs of black clothing, not just because they didn't go with 98% of my clothes, but because I didn't feel myself when I was wearing black. Colour has been proven to have a powerful influence over our moods countless times, and as I decided back then:

Life is far too short to wear things that don't reflect who you are.

The exact same principle applies to your home. It is a living thing, somewhere you should feel your most comfortable and content, so you shouldn't be compromising on the colours that make you feel like *you*.

Nothing brought home the power of colour more to me than when we had to renovate. When we bought our house, it was awash with dull brown carpets, beige lino, and faded apricot anaglypta five layers thick – not many people's idea of a dream interior aesthetic.

Fast forward four years, through enough dust and debris to rival a small tornado, and I can scarcely believe it is the same building I fell in love with – *despite its many quirks* – back in 2019. Gone is the incoherent mishmash of a scheme, replaced with a palette of colours that warms my heart, soothes my soul, and is a pleasure to come home to every day. We didn't carry out any extensive architectural changes on some *Grand Designs*-style budget.

It is purely down to the power of colour.

Colour can take an unremarkable, lifeless space devoid of any personality, and transform it into your personal haven. Once you identify the colours that you connect with, you can set about crafting these into the fabric of your home. Whether you want to energize your hallway, create a serene setting in your office, or a welcoming atmosphere in your living room – colour is the tool you require to free these feelings and express your individuality.

HOW COLOUR MAKES YOUR HOME YOUR OWN

'The best rooms have something to say about the people who live in them.' **David Hicks, interior designer**

One of the first things I ask people who come to me for interior advice is *'what is your favourite colour, and why do you love it?'* I know it sounds almost stupidly simplistic, the kind of thing you might ask a child when you're stuck for a conversation topic other than *Peppa Pig*. But far too many people profess that their favourite colour is... let's say green, for example, and then you take a look at their home and what do you find? Not one iota of green, in any of its guises. A stretch of 'fashionable' grey as far as the eye can see, but the colour they profess to love the most? Not a sausage.

You should view your home as your sanctuary. **What do you love? What makes you feel content and happy?** Your emotions and your colour preferences are intrinsically linked – once you take the time to perceive how certain colours make you feel, you can then create a palette that will simultaneously bring you joy and tell your story.

Think about your happiest moments – sitting in your grandma's terracotta kitchen adorned with sunflowers, the blue of the sea on a day by the coast, or your dad's favourite olive-green fishing jumper. Using colours inspired by your fondest memories will ensure you feel welcomed when you come home, and create a foundation upon which to build your home's interior palette.

The absolute number one piece of advice I can offer to anyone embarking on an interior project would be:

Do not decorate according to trends. Ever. Full stop.

That is a sure-fire way to suck the life and personality out of your home and ensure you will be back out with the paintbrushes in six months' time – and let's face it, painting isn't a task you want to be doing twice a year. If you follow trends obsessively, you are setting yourself up to fail. The happiest and most welcoming houses reflect their owners; their passions, memories and sense of humour, all wrapped up in colours. They make the house feel loved and in turn make you as a guest feel welcome, intrigued to know more. So stay true to the colours that resonate with you, and you won't go wrong.

TIME TO DEMYSTIFY COLOUR

The science behind how humans perceive colour is extensive, multi-faceted and, quite frankly, mind-blowing. The first recorded use of the colour red was over 75,000 years ago, so it's fair to say that colour has been on quite a lengthy journey. There are libraries' worth of volumes that take a deep dive into the way our brains receive and process colour, through the light spectrum.

Now, I'm not a scientist, so I'm not going to attempt to wow you with my methodical breakdown of the colour spectrum – although if you do require more comprehensive technical insight, Sir Isaac Newton had a pretty profound grasp of the idea. He is the reason our current rainbow consists of seven colours – indigo and orange were his additions to the party back in 1704. *Cheers Isaac!*

Instead, I am here to help guide you with some practical knowledge, based on compiling colour schemes that will not only work for you, but also make the most of your home.

Colour has suffered a somewhat tarnished reputation over the years.

Even before the 90s and its clashing sickly purple walls on a certain interior design programme (you know the one), colour was sometimes viewed as childish, garish and even, dare I say it, tacky...

But, there has been a colour revolution.

It is no longer *only* acceptable to adorn your home in safe muted tones, which was the general consensus for most. In the last 10 years a kaleidoscope of paint colours have burst into our otherwise beige lives – bringing with them the opportunity to create homes filled to the brim with every tint, shade and tone. And skipping into the paint aisle to check out these vivid and exciting hues has come a newly emerged community of colour enthusiasts, championing the use of a more stimulating palette. New and historic paint companies alike have added innovative, colourful shades to their repertoires, meaning colour is no longer something to shy away from.

If you have been holding back from using the colours you love, now is the time to change that habit and break the cycle of settling for less than what makes you happy; we have never had better resources to do so.

Using your fondest memories, emotional connections and unadulterated love for certain colours, you can now begin to craft the colour palette for your home. Because if you are committing to the colours you truly love, **there really is nothing to be scared of**.

02

IDENTIFYING
YOUR PALETTE

Now we've discussed why you should love colour (welcome to the colour club – we have jazzy jackets...), it's time for the best part – the *pièce de résistance* – selecting the beautiful colours for your home. But before you grab the nearest colour card to peruse, remember:

You need to nail down how you want your home to <u>feel</u>.

I lived on a very busy main road growing up, which didn't exactly make for top-notch child-friendly outdoor playtime. Instead, for entertainment I spent the majority of my time drawing, writing and, most of all, reading. Every weekend, my mum and I would make a trip to the local library – *my favourite place in the world*.

The building itself was absolutely nothing to write home about, but what it contained was truly my dreamland.

Come Saturday morning, I would wander the tall shelves, run my hand over the technicolour spines and try to narrow down my selection. I vividly remember I was allowed to check out just six books at once, which seems plenty now, but at the time six books would only take me a few days to read – the joys of being a child with no mundane adult chores – so I had to be picky. I recall how delighted I was surrounded by a rainbow of the happiest-looking books, filled with adventures in far-off lands, and hilariously badly-behaved pets.

The colours of the library shelves, the sense of contentment, and the joy I felt every Saturday when I walked through those doors – that right there was exactly how I desired my house to feel. I wanted it to welcome you in to enjoy a brew, curl up on the couch with a biscuit (or three) and feel completely untroubled by the worries of the day – exactly the way I do.

And how did I achieve the ultimate ambience? Through a magic palette of my <u>most-loved colours</u>.

Stop for a minute, and think about the sort of feeling you wish to create within your rooms. These considerations will guide you to the hues you should choose.

Coveting a space that is fresh, airy and tranquil? Soft lighter shades in natural colours such as green and blue open up a room and allow it to breathe. Dreaming of a cosy and comfortable haven? Warm muted tones of pink, terracotta and sand cocoon your space in a rosy glow. Or perhaps you crave a home that oozes moody glamour? Decadent deep jewel tones of teal, amethyst and onyx will add layers of luxurious character. Take some time to note down the climate you want to create in your home, and which colours you naturally associate with this – remember, your home should reflect *you* and your loves. Once you have these ideas and memories compiled, it's time to consult the workhorse of the chromatic world – our faithful friend, **the colour wheel**.

THE COLOUR WHEEL

I'm a bit of a history enthusiast, so let's take a brief journey back over 300 years, to when colour as we know it was revolutionized. Though colour has existed through every civilization, it was Sir Isaac Newton's experiment with a shaft of light and a prism in a shadowy room that gave birth to the concept of a colour spectrum.

Light is colour, and colour is light.

The two are the same, and one cannot exist without the other (which is why I'm always going on about how important it is to consider your light, but we'll get to that later). Newton identified and defined the colours shown through the prism into seven hues that form the rainbow with which we're all now familiar. Though over the centuries artists, philosophers and scientists have undertaken a plethora of studies into colour, Newton's colour wheel *still* forms the foundation of all colour learnings three centuries later. Because of him we understand how colour relationships form and work to create the beautiful palettes that stop us in our tracks every day – a pretty phenomenal achievement.

Now I know that a lot of people panic when it comes to picking out a colour scheme. I've seen their faces. You're in the local DIY store, and alongside you in the paint aisle is someone staring blankly at the mass of rainbow sample cards.

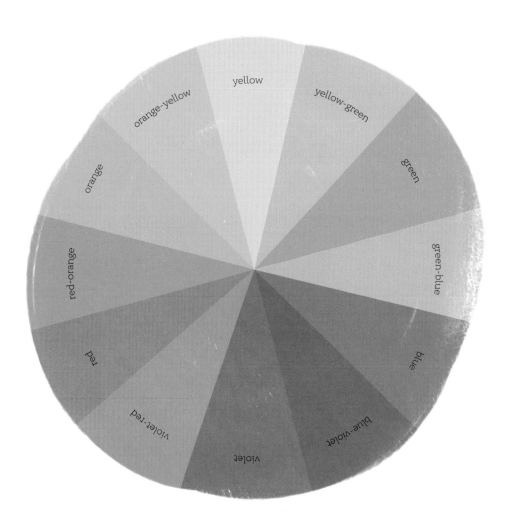

Primary colours

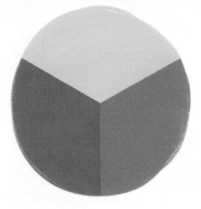

Secondary colours

Tertiary colours

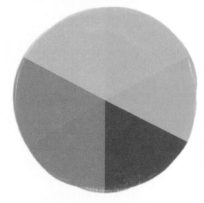

So much choice. *Too much choice* in fact – decision paralysis sets in. The issue is that most people have a colour that they *love* and want to use in their interiors, but they're at a loss as to how to create a colour scheme that works with it. This is where an understanding of the colour wheel comes into play.

Now I'm sure a lot of you will know a touch about colour wheels but we'll start with the basics.

PRIMARY COLOURS

You'll find red, blue and yellow – the primary colours – spaced equidistantly on the colour wheel. These cannot be made by mixing any other colours together. I always picture a box of wax crayons when I think of primary colours – bright and fun-loving.

SECONDARY COLOURS

The offspring of two primary colours when they are combined: green, purple and orange – the ultimate 70s chic trio.

TERTIARY COLOURS

When you mix a secondary colour with its nearest primary neighbour, a tertiary colour is born. Blue-green, red-violet, and yellow-orange just to name a few – the complete technicolour package.

These three groups are the colour-equivalent of your bread and butter; the blocks that make up the very being of the colour wheel. When it comes to creating your colour palette, you need to know *what goes with what* (something I realize a lot of people struggle with and for that you need to get acquainted with colour families.

I'd just like to preface the next section by saying that even though this information aims to help you make informed decisions and avoid having a paint crisis in a DIY store, when it comes to colour, there is no such thing as rules – more like guidelines. A lot of clashing colours in a home can be viewed as chaotic, but some people thrive in chaos – it makes them happy – and if this is you, throw caution to the wind. I salute you! I, however, prefer a more serene, harmonious setting to calm my whirlwind mind. Following these guidelines for pairing congruous colours can help you achieve that too.

Welcome to the colour families – there are only two key ones, and a bit like the Montagues and Capulets, they are on opposing sides.

WARM COLOURS

Red, orange, yellow and every tertiary shade that exists between them make up the warm branch of the colour wheel family tree. Think terracotta pots radiating the heat of an Italian summers' day; a harlequin sunflower growing in your garden; the flesh of a fresh watermelon in your salad. These energizing warm hues are known to advance towards you in a space, and can help make a large deserted room feel cosy and bijou. They are also fantastic at warming up your home – exactly the reason I chose yellow walls for our north-facing kitchen.

COOL COLOURS

On the other side of the colour coin are the cool members of the family: green, blue and purple, and every tertiary shade in between. The colour of watery patches of sky in autumn; birch leaves casting dappled light on your woodland walk; the violet *lobelia* you saw climbing the walls outside the church grounds. These hues are the antithesis of the warm side and so, rather than advancing towards you, they give the illusion of space – pushing your walls and ceiling outwards to allow a room to breathe. They can calm your home, lending an air of tranquillity and peace.

Although these are the colour families split into their simplest form, you need to remember that **each colour has warm- and cool-shade varieties, even neutrals**. This means you don't have to discount a colour just because it doesn't fit into the family you desire; you just have to ensure you choose the correct *shade*.

It's all about the undertones.
Take blue for example. I'm a huge admirer of Monet, who had the incredible power to harness both sides of a colour's potential. In *The Fisherman's House at Varengeville*, the cerulean blue of the ocean, paired with the soft periwinkle of the summer sky means you can practically feel the balmy heat of the day radiating from the scene. Contrast this with the blues in *The Cote Sauvage*, a cold Aegean sea muddled with a steely denim shade, and a brisk sea breeze blows from the image. While both scenes are blue, the summery warm blues are yellow toned, whereas the chilly cold-looking blues contain much more purple undertones.

Now you have this knowledge, your eye will start to see these undertones when you are comparing colours, and you'll soon have it down to a fine art. You'll no longer have to stand bewildered, weighing up sample cards; instead you'll be able to spend this time on more pleasant pursuits, such as eating cake.

No chat on the colour wheel would be complete without a little side note on **complementary colours**.

It is always said that opposites attract, and the same goes for colours.

Pink and green, yellow and blue... these are matches made in heaven. You might have wondered why, when you bring daffodils into your blue kitchen, they suddenly look even brighter and happier! That's because blue and yellow shades sit opposite each other on the colour wheel, and a colour's opposite brings out its best, making each one more vibrant.

Complementary colours are one of my favourite schemes to use – who doesn't want to get the most out of their colours?

WHICH COLOURS & WHY

Colour is all down to perception, and each one of us views a colour differently. We all have hues that we *naturally* gravitate towards.

Consider your wardrobe, your choice in artwork, the shades that catch your eye as you walk down the street.

These associations are a result of memories you have formed and retained through the years, and they all link back to specific colours. For instance, whenever I see a certain tone of sky blue, I always think of a particular T-shirt my mum *constantly* wears – and it makes me smile. Having positive memories of certain colours and using these in your home will ensure you always receive a warm welcome when you come through the door.

Our memories of treasured times are ideal for helping us unlock the colours that make us the happiest. These might be moments from childhood, or from wonderful holidays – a place you visited and subsequently fell in love with. The pinkish light of a Scottish sky at golden hour; the lilac hydrangeas growing round the shore of Lake Garda; the aquamarine ice-cold water of the Soča river. Using memories to identify the colours you love is a perfect way to start orchestrating your home's colour palette. Once you have a favourite hue in mind, refer back to the colour wheel and use it as a starting point to identify what colours work well with it.

'Be faithful to your own taste, because nothing you really like is ever out of style.' **Billy Baldwin, interior designer**

Lighter tints of any colour bestow a calmer, softer atmosphere, whereas deeper shades intensify a room, accomplishing a cosier or moodier feel, depending on the hue. **There is a world of colour to unlock.**

To illustrate, if your most-loved colour is a yellow-toned green, and you crave a harmonious earthy home, try pairing it with other warm-toned shades of its neighbouring colours – **yellow, orange and blue**.

Or perhaps you fancy something a little more bold and out there? Go for complementary tones of **warm pinks or reds** to bring out the best in both colours, and allow them to shine.

Remember, your colour choices all boil down to two key things:

The mood you want to create, and the colours <u>you</u> love.

It doesn't matter if your friends all have grey living rooms, and they think you should too because it's the 'in' thing – if you have no emotional connection or love for grey, you aren't going to feel like your home represents *you*. Honestly, avoid trends; they dampen a room's true spirit. Instead select colours that speak to you, to ensure a long love affair. People say 'I'd love to have a colourful home but I'm worried I'll go off it', but the truth is, if you really, *truly* love the colours you pick, you won't go off them. I'm not worried about eating my favourite chocolate every day in case I go off it – you know why? Because I bloody love chocolate. It's that simple.

Your favourite colours + the atmosphere you want to create + a moodboard = a magically harmonious home. A myriad of colours awaits you.

MAKING
MOODBOARDS

One of the most valuable instruments in your interior design arsenal is something that can be made relatively quickly, for next to nothing, and requires no skill, yet the assistance it provides is monumental. I know what you're thinking: calm down Jessica, *it's only a moodboard*, but that is where you are wrong, my friend.

I'm someone who is naturally good at visualizing how a space will look once it achieves its full potential, and I won't lie, it's a pretty useful gift. I mean, I'd love to be able to bake something edible, but you can't have it all. Yet not everyone possesses this talent for visualization, and therein lies the issue. If you can't paint a clear picture in your mind of how the colours and layout are going to look in situ, this will make decorating more difficult. *What if the colours don't work*

together? What if that fabric will look too busy in the space? All valid reservations to hold, as when you've gone to the effort of decorating, you want the result to be perfection personified!

Now I can't bestow upon you the power of visualization, but I can help you with the next best thing – creating a tangible display of your ideas *in real life*. Right in front of your eyes. This way, not only can you review, rework and fine-tune your colours, fabrics and finishes, you can also utilize your moodboard to share your ideas with other non-visualizers. Instead of fraught conversations of 'just trust me Brian, the living room will look sensational in pink and orange... I think...' you will be able to demonstrate just how marvellous it's going to be to anyone else you want to get on board the wonderful colour train.

WHAT IS A MOODBOARD?

'The details are
not the details; they
make the design.'
Charles Eames, designer

So, you've got in mind the kind of hues you're looking to use – now it's moodboard time. There are two types you can create, depending on your personal preference and the level of detail you want to get into: physical and digital. I'm a wake-up-in-the-night-worrying-that-I-need-to-move-the-dresser level of perfectionist, so I prefer a hands-on physical moodboard to get into the nitty gritty; to touch and feel the fabrics and to inspect the paint finish up close.

No level of detail is too much for me.

Yet both moodboard concepts have their merits – the digital type takes up zero space, is extremely speedy to put together, and your partner won't roll their eyes when you bring home the 12th new fabric swatch that week.

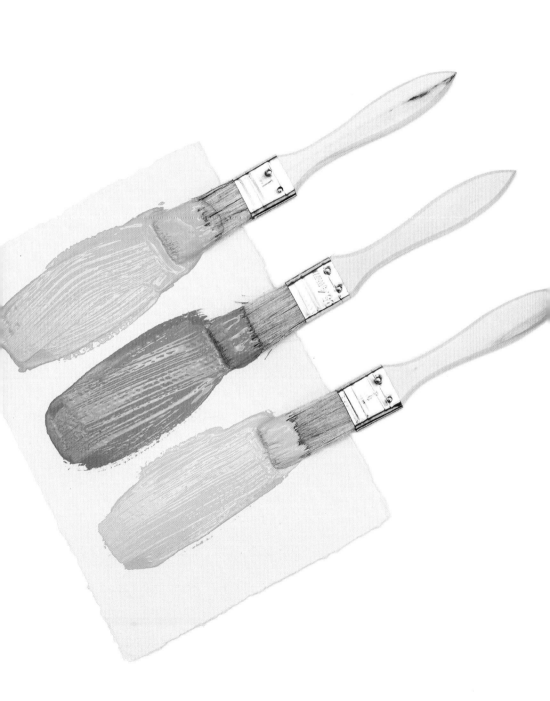

HOW TO MAKE A MOODBOARD & WHAT TO INCLUDE

PHYSICAL

Once you have the colours you are drawn to for your room in mind, gathering the items needed for your moodboard is a little bit like a scavenger hunt.

Let everyday life inspire you.

For the base of the board, I either use an A3 (tabloid) piece of card if I am drawing the space out Art Attack style (more on that later) or a large wooden tray – somewhere that I can store all my samples and keep the elements together.

Now the fun begins!

Paint samples are indispensable when it comes to moodboards, as their colours provide the glorious backdrop to the life that occurs within your rooms, allowing the other elements to sing. Paint your samples onto scraps of paper or card – that way, you can move them off your moodboard and around your room as the day elapses and the light shifts.

Colour cards and paint chips are also great additions to your board; layer them up in your chosen hues, and see how the colours interact with one another.

Then, gather swatches and remnants of fabrics for curtains, cushions, upholstery and other soft furnishings – most fabric, wallpaper and sofa websites allow you to order a handful of free samples, so make the most of this. You can include carpet swatches, table linens, wallpaper snippets, pieces of tile, cabinet hardware, even scraps torn from magazines (I'm bad for this, I always forget I've ripped out the pages when I go back to read the article)... the sky's the limit.

View yourself as the interiors equivalent of a magpie.

Anything whimsical that sparks a feeling of wonder can also go on the board. You aim is to build and curate a collection that either *illustrates the mood behind the colour scheme* you are creating, or that specifically features *what you want to include in the space*, to ensure it ties in with all the other components.

DIGITAL

You can create the modern-day version of the physical board with something as basic as a Word document, or a program such as Canva or Photoshop, if you have the skillset.

All you require is a **blank canvas to pour your ideas on to**. Start by shaping out a rough floor plan of your room or house – or use the whole page as a base for placing your ideas on.

After that, you need to gather your items. Images from Google and Pinterest will help build up your composition; include your ideal room furnishings, cushions and curtains. That ochre velvet sofa you have been coveting online? Onto the board it goes. Anything you would include on a physical board can be included in digital form. Instead of hand-painted samples, you can copy and paste images from the paint brand's website, to layer up your tones and get a feel for the room's overall atmosphere.

As you don't have to leave the comfort of your home to physically gather supplies, digital moodboards are usually a lot quicker to create – though, for me, nothing can beat seeing a paint sample up close in person (I may be obsessed).

To repeat myself, there is no real skill involved with moodboarding; it's an enjoyable game of trial and error, with no downsides. It's almost like creating a collage – but one that will actually assist you rather than just be beautiful to behold. If you don't like the look of something on your board, simply remove it!

The activity of creating a moodboard is to get a *feel* for the relationship between your colours and the physical objects within the rooms, so even if you *can't visualize* how everything will work together, you can now see it in front of you.

HOW TO UTILISE YOUR MOODBOARD

The best thing about creating a moodboard – aside from the hours of craft-like fun (pass me a glue stick and I'm in my element) – is that it allows you to capture *all your interior ideas in one place*. It clearly illustrates how your chosen colours, patterns and textures will complement one another and work in harmonious wonder.

If you struggle with creating colour combinations, your moodboard will enable you to experiment in a risk-free way.

You don't have to implement all the colours into the room and *then* realize you dislike the way saffron orange looks against your beautiful heliotrope chair – your moodboard allows you to discover this way before any paint gets near the walls. Decorating is a time-consuming process; this way, you know that when you do reach the painting stage, you have a plan to follow and refer back to at any point. Most importantly, it's one that **you created and truly love!**

I touched on this earlier, but there are a lot of people who do not possess the power of visualization. Like second sight, though much less creepy, you either have it or you don't.

My grandma is a great visualizer; my mum is terrible. I can't tell you how many times I heard: *'I'm not sure about this Jessica, it looks bloody awful'* during our house renovation. Really fills you with confidence.

Luckily for me I could see the end goal clearly in my mind, and it kept me sane. But what really helped to get others on board with my colourful ideas – and convince them I wasn't completely mad – was the moodboard I created.

If you aren't confident of your ideas, it makes it very difficult to reassure others.

Partners can sometimes require *gentle*, or not so gentle, persuasion to embrace a home that isn't just stark white walls. Once you have your moodboard created, you can clearly show how all the colours, textures and tones will live in harmony together, taking the guess work and stress out of decorating.

Moodboards also make designing your rooms a more collaborative experience, allowing everyone who needs to have a say to input, review and rework the elements – the end product being **a home that everyone loves**.

SKETCHING YOUR ROOM LAYOUT

One of the principal pieces of advice I offer my interior clients, friends, neighbours and anyone who unwittingly asks me a casual question on colour is:

View your house as a whole.

Yes, your home is made up of individual rooms, but if you want that beautiful harmonious flow of colours throughout, you need to consider them as one entity. If you have an interest in interiors, you will likely have come across the term 'the red thread'; this Swedish expression denotes something that follows a theme. This doesn't mean that every one of your rooms needs to look the same; they simply need a detail or concept that creates familiarity and a cohesive feel. For our house, the red thread is the colour palette: **blue, pink, yellow** and **green**.

Yes, these all appear in a myriad of shades, guises and differing ratios, but they are the only four colours I use in the house. This means that even though you aren't *consciously* aware of this, *subconsciously* your brain recognizes the colour similarities as you pass from room to room – generating a feeling of harmony and positive flow, despite the house being filled with a blend of colours.

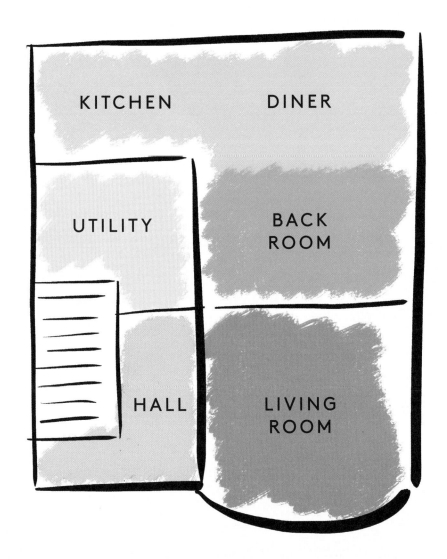

To help you plan out the colour relationships between your rooms, I recommend sketching out the floor plan of your home – it is the perfect backdrop on which to build your moodboard and plan your colour combinations.

Don't worry, this isn't where I spring it upon you that you're going to need that grade in art. I'm rubbish at drawing, but fortunately you don't need to have artistic skills for this – although if you do, it will look fantastic, I'm sure.

Unless you live in an ancestral manor that has been passed down the generations (one can dream), the quickest and easiest way to do this is to find a floor plan of your house on the internet – there will most likely be one on Rightmove, or whichever house-selling site you use, from the last time it sold. Use this image as a guide and draw out the rough outline and room divisions onto a piece of card or paper (I would say A3 size for each floor so you have enough space to plan the rooms properly). Again, you can do this digitally if you're more of a technological whizz. Don't fret if you can't find a floor plan – a very rough outline of the rooms will work just as well.

Once your floor plan has taken shape, start to insert your chosen palette. Paint your samples onto small pieces of paper, or use printed paint cards, and place them into your mapped-out rooms. If you know without doubt that you want your bedroom to be pea green, start there. Then survey your other spaces and see in what ways you can include green into the schemes.

It doesn't have to be anything as dramatic as painting the walls – it could be a **green detailed rug** in your front room, a **verdigris tablecloth** in your kitchen, or an **olive roman blind** in your hallway.

This is why I like to *combine* sketching out the house layout with creating a moodboard, using the floor plan as the perfect backdrop to hone the palette and switch the shades about.

With my physical boards, I print and cut out cushions, curtains and sofas – even my beloved blue log-burning stove was on the first moodboard long before I purchased it. But it isn't only new items you need to add to the moodboard. A moodboard is the ideal place to get a feel for how your existing pieces are going to welcome the new colour scheme. Thus your beautiful sand sofa becomes the perfect backdrop for the new earthy warm tones of terracotta blankets and forest green cushions.

Having your rooms laid out including the new palette allows you to see how the colours cooperate and flow from one to the next. Go on working and reworking the hues until you feel completely content.

Ultimately the board will become your home's interior map and a colourful journey awaits!

COLOUR
SCHEMES

'One can speak poetry, just by arranging colour well.'
Vincent Van Gogh, artist

So, you've identified the colours you love and connect with, started work compiling your moodboard... *however*, you're feeling a little stuck about what other hues to pair with them. As I briefly mentioned at the beginning of this book, **colour is everywhere**; ergo, so is inspiration for your colour palette!

I promise – you just have to think a little outside of the box.

My love affair with colour is a long one; I covet, admire and relish it, especially when it appears incongruously. A huge patch of lilac asters growing in abundance on wasteland; a weathered, neglected backstreet door in the perfect shade of buttery yellow; a sudden and unexpected burst of colour that makes you stop as you pass by, and really take notice. It takes me longer to get to places, granted, but I can't help myself. Colour in these situations serves as a tool to elevate something mundane into something magical. Nowhere on the planet (that I have yet to find, and trust me, I've looked) encompasses this more than the Italian island of Burano. Situated in the dreamy Venetian Lagoon, this minute fisherman's island is almost entirely filled with residential houses, interwoven with canals that snake through its centre. The island is quaint and the surrounding sea views are stunning, but what really sets Burano apart is the **colour**.

Every single home and building is a different delicious shade: soft apricot merges to coral, followed closely by mint, sea foam, tangerine and lavender. It is a technicolour feast for the eyes, at every turn a fresh set of colours rushes to greet you.

We stayed on the island a couple of years ago, in a magnificent fuchsia house with bottle-green shutters, which allowed us to experience the true beauty of Burano. Before the first vaporetto of tourists arrived from Venice each morning, I would head out into the freezing air of a February sunrise – blue skied and breathtaking. For that hour or so I wouldn't meet a soul; it was just me and the local swans drinking in the wondrous colours the island offers. I would perch on the bridges, survey the sunrise and marvel at how the hues of the houses worked alongside each other. One colourful building is wonderful, but a *whole island* formed from a rainbow of colours is quite spectacular. Van Gogh said 'there is no blue without yellow, and without orange', meaning that *colours truly sing when they are paired with complementary others*. A sublime colour palette is to your home what a majestic view is to your eyes.

Undiluted happiness.

I have compiled the following examples of palettes to hopefully assist and inspire you in your colour quest. You'll find everything from cool neutrals to jewel tones, because believe it or not I do love all colours – yes, even you brown – and think they deserve to live in your home.

PASTELS

Blush. Forget-me-not. Pale lilac. Sorbet yellow.
Mint. Peach blossom. Cotton white. Pistachio.
Sherbet orange. Mallow pink. Sea glass green.
Wedgwood blue. Lemon. Powder blue.

My first love – pastels are perfect for people who love soft muted shades but still want a colour hit. Not just for children's bedrooms, they are essentially full colours with more tint (white) added – allowing you to create the impact of a colourful home on a more toned-down scale.

TOP TIP

To avoid a pastel scheme looking too sugary or childish, add natural and raw elements into your room: an oiled wooden floor, a vintage rattan light shade or a bamboo sideboard.

You could also include a darker rug or artwork into the mix, something that sits well with your chosen pastels but provides a deeper-toned background colour to really ground the space. So, if your room is a soft pink, go for a deep burgundy rug that includes lighter tones. Pastels have an overly sweet reputation (which I disagree with) so you want to counterbalance this – throw something into the room that people won't expect. Nobody wants everything to match anyway – you aren't creating a show home after all!

BRIGHTS

Acid yellow. Bottle green. Cobalt blue. Candy pink.
Sixties mauve. Tangerine. Pillar box red. Turquoise.
Sky blue. Lime. Hot pink. Marigold. Coral.
Absinthe green. Scarlet. Electric blue. Violet.

The colour wheel turned up to 150% is where the bright colours live. Bold and beautiful, these hues don't so much welcome you as greet you with a flamboyant cheer. Brights are equal parts striking and alluring – even people who don't profess to be colour lovers can't help but be curious. If you crave interiors that pack a punch, these colours are for you.

TOP TIP

In my opinion, brights should either be used to create an all-in wow-factor scheme, or to add a minimal accent pop of colour – no middle ground. Because they are delightful and daring, that is exactly how they should be used – to be bold and create *drama*. If bright colours are your thing, go for it – *I mean really go for it*. Walls and ceiling adorned in an electric hue will elevate your rooms from everyday to exceptional. No one will forget them. Conversely, an equally powerful way to utilize a bright is to use it to add an accent pop of colour in an otherwise neutral space. Like a lighthouse beacon in a storm, painting just one element in your room a show-stopping shade will allow it to shine as a fearless focal point. Your staircase, your ceiling, even your window reveal – pick your favourite feature and highlight it with the boldest colours around.

JEWEL

Deep teal. Kingfisher blue. Amethyst. Claret pink.
Peridot. Rich burgundy. Emerald. Citrine. Gold.
Royal purple. Sapphire. Lapiz blue. Tanzanite
lavender. Tourmaline green. Copper. Garnet.

Classy and opulent, jewel tones are the perfect way to add a touch of elegance and mystery to your home. Because of their rich nature, they can make a room feel warmer, luxurious and more intimate, creating an aspiring *Great Gatsby*-esque atmosphere – and let's face it, who doesn't wish they could have experienced the grandiose ways of the roaring twenties?

TOP TIP

If you long for your rooms to envelop you in a lavish embrace, and adore things on the darker side, jewel tones are your new best friends. To create the perfect jewel aesthetic, you want to carefully consider your accent metals: taps, cupboard and door handles, even light switches – they may seem like trivial pieces in the grand scheme of your home, but as they say, darling, the devil is in the detail. The rich atmosphere of these colours warrants warmer metal shades of brass, bronze, copper and gold to allow them to *really* shine – after all, that's what jewels do best.

EARTH

Rust red. Forest green. Terracotta. River blue. Shell pink. Sand. Pebble grey. Olive. Bark. Fawn. Honey yellow. Moss. Truffle brown. Pearl. Seafoam. Clay. Spruce green. Mushroom. Deep sea.

No colours bring home nature more than harmonious earthy hues. With warm brown undertones, earth colours reflect calmness, tranquillity and a serene kind of solitude. Imagine walking through a woodland heading for the coast. Dappled light surrounds you as the red sun beats down and, just ahead, a bank of tidal pools breaches the sand – dark rocky troughs filled to the brim with glittering seawater and kelp. These are the colours that connect with the natural world the most – so if the outdoors is where you find peace, earth tones are ideal for your home.

TOP TIP

One of the simplest schemes to imbue in your interiors, an earthy palette will come naturally to most. Earth tones ground your rooms; they are inherently calming colours, helping you feel more connected with nature, and bringing the sense of the outside in. No drama, no nonsense, these colours settle peacefully into the fabric of your home – always radiating a bucolic atmosphere but never vying for too much attention. Go for the hues that really speak to you – whether that be a home of mountainside greens and greys, or my personal favourite, freshwater blue with a hint of rusty red. Colour poetry in motion.

DARK

Shadow. Ink black. Merlot. Coal. Truffle. Onyx. Twilight. Shark grey. Copper beech. Obsidian. Jet. Incarnadine. Umber. Ebony. Blue black. Espresso. Chocolate brown. Kohl. Cocoa bean.

Between mystery and midnight is where the dark colours reside. These hues are the antithesis of pastels, with a lot more *shade* added in order to achieve their deep and intense levels of colour. Moody and alluring, darker tones cocoon your rooms with a feeling that lighter ones just cannot achieve. True black may be defined by the absence of colour, but there is a vast array of dark shades out there that are sure to satisfy anyone with a taste for the dark side.

TOP TIP

One of the main things that people say puts them off from using dark colours is that they don't want to make their room feel small and dingy. Granted,

'Bat-Cave Chic' is not an interior aesthetic most people are looking for, so how do you avoid this? Like all colour conundrums, it's all about the undertones (shocking I know). If your rooms are north facing, sticking a load of blue-toned black on the walls is going to leave you feeling frosty and gloomy – so counterbalance that cold northern light with a rich and enigmatic dark brown, leaving your room a cocoon of warmth and intrigue while still delivering that dark look you covet. Dark colours done right curate a feeling of intimacy and warmth, so pair them with other deep elements such as classic wooden furniture or flooring to finish your scheme off perfectly.

WARM NEUTRALS

Faded terracotta. Plaster pink. Linen. Nude. Beige.
Oyster white. Taupe. Mink brown. Straw yellow.
Sandstone. Washed clay. Leather brown. Canvas.
Ivory. Buff. Putty. Milk white. Limewash.

Fear not, warm neutrals have nothing to do with the long-out-of-favour magnolia of the past. Delicious soft natural shades – the kind of colours you would describe as muted or dusky – the warm side of the neutral family leans towards yellow, pink or brown undertones, yet with enough grey in there to ensure they don't tip over into 'cream' territory.

TOP TIP

Delicate and sophisticated, these pale almost 'non colours' are ideal if you want to create a minimal aesthetic, but *still* crave that feeling of warmth and cosiness. Influenced by their earthy undertones, these airy and light shades bestow a mellow and inviting atmosphere. The colour equivalents of linen voile curtains blowing in a soft summer breeze – bliss! To keep a harmonious feel, make sure you stick to neutrals from the same family – for example, plaster, shell and oyster white all share a pink-brown undertone.

COOL NEUTRALS

Slate grey. Cloud white. Birch. Ash. Silver. Shadow white. Dove. Morning light. Pale smoke. Salt. Marble. Fog grey. Lead. Ice. Drizzle. Brilliant white. Steel grey. Moon white. Chalk. Whitewash.

Born from black and grey origins, cool-toned neutrals are the paler, softer offspring of these crisp hues. They're similar to warm neutrals in the sense that they don't have a very strong 'colour' on first inspection, but that is where any similarities come to an abrupt end. Fresh, clean and brisk, these are the neutrals you call upon when you want to achieve a modern and minimal interior.

TOP TIP

If you adore contemporary interiors, yet don't want a strong hit of colour, cool neutrals may be the tones for you. Naturally colder with blue or purple undertones, they will suit southern-facing rooms without feeling too clinical. Alternatively, if a stark or cleaner atmosphere is what you love, these tones will only be enhanced by cooler northern-facing light. The perfect palette for a modern décor home.

05

DON'T BE AFRAID OF THE DARK

Nyctophilia: A love of the dark; Finding relaxation or comfort in the darkness.

Black. A truly mercurial beast. On one hand, its cultural associations are strongly tied to mortality, misery and despair. The **Black** Death. A **black** day. The **Black** Dog. Yet on the other – evening glove-bedecked – hand, black is seen as chic, the pinnacle of high fashion and the epitome of class. Whatever regard you hold for black and its other deep sister shades, there is no question that using a dark colour scheme in your home can be *completely and positively transformative*. Some people are under the impression that if you have a small room lacking natural light, the best thing you can do is whack a load of brilliant white on the walls to brighten up the space. When they tell me about their grand white-emulsion plans, I'm sure my cries of, NO PLEASE DON'T DO THAT, can be heard from streets away. **Remember, colour is light**; for a pale colour to perform to its full potential, it needs light – no amount of white paint is going to transform your dimly-lit room into a cathedral of illumination. Instead, it's often wiser to lean into the dark. Darker shades are mysterious and dramatic, a bit like a majestic peacock – and similar to peacocks, some people are a bit scared of them. They think they're beautiful to behold but are unsure how to fit them into their homes (the colours, not the birds). But there are so many wonderful dark shades out there just waiting to become the perfect match for your cosy intimate corners. If you're ready to embrace the dark side, step this way.

HOW TO EMBRACE DARK TONES IN YOUR HOME

Dark colours tend to all get lumped into the same murky category, when in reality there is as much variation within the dark hues family as any other. If someone told me they wanted a dark colour palette for their home, I wouldn't just hand them a tin of black paint and wave them off. While one person might seek a clean, cool and classic dark home, another might want a cosy and sumptuous feeling with rich warm shades. As with choosing any colour scheme, it's all about how you want your home to *feel*. If you're a night owl who loves to entertain with flair,

crave mystery and drama in your space, or want to create a cocooning environment in which to unwind, blacks and other dark colours will be ideal for your home.

As with all colours, dark shades can be tailored for any kind of home environment; your space, tastes and, most importantly, light will determine how these tones work best in your home. As lighting is the most important factor, I've split it down into the following to make life simpler.

EMBRACING THE DARK IN A ROOM WITH LOTS OF LIGHT

If you love deep moody hues, and your rooms contain large windows, skylights or other elements that allow natural light to flood in – congratulations, your decorating job just became that bit easier. I mean, the room isn't going to paint itself, but the colour selection process will be more straightforward, and your walls will be able to tolerate the darkest of darks. Rooms that benefit from large amounts of natural light cooperate with dark colours effortlessly.

Dark colours advance towards you, which can make a room feel smaller, but an abundance of light helps colours shine to their full potential (remember that colour = light), allowing you to really run wild and go as dark as you like without worrying about shrinking your space.

TO NOTE

If your room faces south, that is the interiors equivalent of a green tick for any shade, as the light will be warm and complementary to all colours. North-facing light is a lot cooler, so pick dark hues with warm undertones such as yellow or red to stop your room feeling too hostile.

EMBRACING THE DARK IN A ROOM LACKING IN LIGHT

If you live in a cottage, or any kind of home where your windows are on the diminutive side, natural light may be in short supply, which can stop colours from appearing true. Instead, you could be left with murky, cold shadows of their former selves. To counteract this, err on the side of richer and warmer shades such as chocolate brown, dense rusty red or blacks with these as their undertone – they will still deliver a dark punch but also imbue plenty of warmth into your space. Although restricted amounts of natural light are viewed as less favourable, darker homes adopt a moody palette with ease – making it simple to create your dream soothing heaven.

TO NOTE

If your room receives low light, colours that look relatively bright elsewhere will appear *a lot* darker – so consider going for a shade lighter than your 'ideal', as once it's on your walls, it will appear deeper and more intense. If you go too dark, it can leave an already shadowy room feeling cave-like.

EARTHY DARKS

Dark olive green.
Deep chocolate.
Understated taupe.

Earthy comforting shades of rich deep greens can fill your home with a sense of solace and calm. Team these with tonal shades of chocolate brown, soft plaster and taupe to add a sense of depth and interest. The lighter sandy tones will help to emphasize the warmth within the dark green, and keep your space feeling grounded.

This kind of colour scheme is perfect for those who crave a dark space but aren't ready to take the plunge into inky black tones; or those who love a natural palette, but want one with more of a sumptuous, rich feel to it – like a walk through an ancient forest at dusk.

COOL DARKS

Blue-black. True navy.
Cool white.

A blue toned black on your walls
will provide a clean and classic
backdrop to the space – paired
with a pure snow white and a
deeply saturated sapphire blue
to really achieve that timeless
look. Think classic dark Victorian-
esque atmosphere; deep navy
inky walls, topped with ornate
bone-white cornice, ebony and
ivory checkerboard floors, deep
charcoal Gothic sash windows
and a black cast iron fireplace,
complete with roaring fire – cool-
toned perfection!

This type of scheme is ideal for
those who crave a classic dark
interior, and who prefer their
paint colours on the fresher side.
In a south-facing space, these
blue tones will balance out the
warmer light and still manage
to leave your room feeling airy
and crisp.

WARM DARKS

Red-black. Rich burgundy. Muted pink

Crave dark, glamourous and dramatic, but not necessarily 'black-black'? Consider deep burgundy, mysterious clarets and brown-pinks, which all instil warmth, enveloping the room in a rosy dark cocoon, whilst still providing a glow of colour.

Contemplate russets and wines with a delicate smattering of a lighter, dusty rose – romantic, opulent and sumptuous; who wouldn't want their room to feel like this? A red-based black palette is exactly the sort of scheme required for those of you who have your heart set on keeping your interiors charming and soft, whilst still embracing the darker side of decor.

TOP TIPS FOR YOUR PERFECT DARK SPACE

- **Like all colours, dark hues are still all about undertones.** If you've fallen for a cool charcoal, pair this with other blue-toned shades, such as a true black and crisp white for a harmonious scheme. In love with a deep mahogany? Choose lighter shades of warm browns and rusts to complement it.

- **If your room is feeling a little on the dingy side due to low light, mirrors are your friend!** They will bounce light around the room, mimicking a large window. To make the best use of them, place a mirror opposite a window or next to your lamps to maximize the glow.

- **Love the dark, but want to avoid your room becoming too shadowy?** Balance the deep tones with lighter colours – from a fresh white, to a mousey grey or pale rose. Not only will this stop your room feeling too dark, it will also add a delicious contrast.

- **Texture is key – you want to include lots of contrasts to add that feel of luxe**: wood, rattan, velvet, wool, mixed metals. Layer these textures across your soft furnishings and accessories to help provide contrast with your dark colours, and stop things looking two dimensional.

- **While pale and cool colours make a room feel airy as they appear to recede, darker and warmer colours advance towards you in a space.** Therefore, if you want to make a large desolate room feel cosy and more compact, choose deep mellow hues such as oak browns and jam reds.

- **If you want to elevate your dark colours and add extra 'wow'**, paint a piece of furniture, such as a bookcase, in a high-gloss dark shade; the light bouncing off the lacquered surface will bring an extra element of interest and light to your space.

- **Dark tones are synonymous with elegance.** To tie in with your moody walls and create an opulent feel, choose curtains in a thick heavy fabric with a classic pattern, to add an extra dimension of luxury.

NO SUCH
THING AS
WHITE

'White is the presence of all colours.' **Mary Balogh, writer**

'And for the ceiling, I just want a *nice normal white*.' A sentenced uttered by many, and one that makes me smile every time. *Just* – that tiny word that always seems to prefix a decision on white paint. It makes it sound like all other colours are awkward and problematic to select (from the many, *many* options), but with white there's only one tin on the shelf and he's good for everyone – whatever your lighting conditions or surrounding wall colours. I would *love* to tell you that this was the case – it would certainly have made this a very short chapter to write – but, alas, this is not the way it works. Gone are the days when you could just grab a pot of brilliant white emulsion from your local hardware store.

We are now lucky enough to have a plethora of beautiful white shades at our fingertips; hundreds for every type of light direction and colour family. But instead of seeing this as a bonus, too many people become overwhelmed in an avalanche of sample cards. 'Do I need Ivory Whisper? Alabaster Breeze? What about Snow Drift?' It seems bewildering, but once you approach your decision on white paints using the same method you use for selecting <u>any</u> other colour, you'll have this in the bag. Your rooms will sing once your glorious colours are matched up with their perfect milky counterparts and you're no longer settling for a jarring white in your oasis. Because let's be honest, if the photograph on the next page illustrates anything, it's that there really is **no such thing as white**.

UNDERSTANDING PIGMENTS & UNDERTONES

As with every other colour in the *universe* of interiors, it's all about the undertones. Yes, that fateful word that almost makes you sound like you're in some kind of elusive and elite club of colour knowledge, but in reality it's very easy to understand when you know what you're looking for.

White paints are essentially colours in their most tinted – AKA <u>lightest</u> – form.

There are very few whites in the world that are pure white, which means at the base of your white paint lurks the actual origin colour. Still very much present, but hiding in plain sight and masquerading as white. It could be blue, which means your white will be very bright, cool and crisp – ideal for a modern minimalist abode.

It could be red, giving your white a soft and earthy appearance – the kind of timeless and forgiving shade that would be seen in a stately home. Or perhaps yellow, meaning your white will be on the warmer end of the scale – ideal to fill your space with the paint equivalent of a summer breeze. This information that all whites aren't created equal isn't intended to overwhelm you – on the contrary, I simply believe that after you have gone to the effort of choosing the perfect palette for your home, picking the wrong white is essentially undoing all your hard work. It's like cooking a delicious meal and then just before you serve it, tipping tomato ketchup all over it, because it's a sauce that everyone uses. Does it go? Possibly, but most likely it's just spoilt your food; the same thing goes for your rooms.

THE PAPER TEST

If you think you've found a white you love, but you're not sure if it will marry with the other colours in your scheme or the atmosphere you want to create, there is an easy way to check the undertone. Take a piece of white A4 paper, and lay your sample cards on top. You'll now be able to see that in comparison to the bleached paper, the white you were sure was 'normal' looks like another colour altogether. Note the undertone – is it red and subtle, or grey and stark?

Make sure you carry out this activity in <u>the room you intend to use the white paint in</u>, as you want to be sure you're happy with the way the hue appears in the space's natural light. And this goes for *any* kind of paint sampling. It is absolutely futile testing samples in your living room that faces south, and then heading off to paint your north-facing bedroom and wondering why on earth it now looks so different. **Light is everything when it comes to paint.**

LIGHTING CHECK

I'm know I'm starting to sound like a stuck record, but the most important part of choosing any colour is making sure you know what light you are dealing with. If your room faces south, the light it receives is direct and warm, meaning that it can tolerate even a cool white and still look rather neutral.

The opposite happens in a north-facing room with its blue reflected light, meaning that a white with any kind of cool base, such as grey or purple, will appear amplified. If your rooms are east or west facing, they either receive direct sunlight in the morning or evening – so consider when you will be spending most of your time in there.

If you happen to live in the southern hemisphere, this is all the other way around; just flip the narrative. You can almost view your decision like an equation (never thought I'd be referencing dreaded maths but here we are) – once you know what kind of white you want, you just have to balance it against your light!

SOUTH-FACING
LIGHT

+

BLUE-BASED
WHITE

=

A BALANCED
NEUTRAL
WHITE

SOUTH-FACING
LIGHT

+

YELLOW-BASED
WHITE

=

A WARM
YELLOW
APPEARANCE

NORTH-FACING
LIGHT

+

BLUE-BASED
WHITE

=

A COLD
PALE BLUE
APPEARANCE

NORTH-FACING
LIGHT

+

YELLOW-BASED
WHITE

=

A BALANCED
NEUTRAL
WHITE

HOW TO CHOOSE THE RIGHT WHITE

DECIDE WHAT SORT OF WHITE YOU WANT

If you've gone for an array of terracottas and pinks for your colour palette, you're going to want a warm soft white to tie in with these shades. On the other hand, a mix of icy blues and greys will warrant a cooler, cleaner white, to allow the colours to truly shine. Take time to consider your other colours and how you want the room to feel; once you know what kind of white you're looking for, it's on to step two.

CHECK THE DIRECTION

Stand facing the window and use the compass on your phone (or a separate compass) to see which direction it faces, and make a note for each room. If you know you want a warm white, yet your room faces north, you're going to have to select a slightly more yellow-toned white than your ideal, so it can balance out with the cool blue light your room receives. Remember, it's all an equation of equilibrium – if the light is cool, go warmer (or vice versa) to achieve your perfect outcome. For an east- or west-facing room where the light changes hourly, consider when you will be using it most and if this marries up with when it receives sun.

An east-facing room in the evening is basically a north-facing one (no direct light), so employ the same tactics. Once you have noted all your rooms' light directions, you can now start the paint-sample hunt!

TEST THE SHADE

Gather together the white samples you think will be perfect for your space, and lay them onto a piece of standard white A4 paper. Make sure you do this in the room the samples are destined for – *it's all about the light, remember?* As the paper is bleached, it will allow the undertone colours of your samples to shine through more clearly – have a look over them and decide which evokes the feeling you are looking for. You can also bring in swatches of other colours from your palette to see which white works best in conjunction with them. Once you have chosen one, paint a large sample onto a piece of paper – ensuring no background paper colour is visible – and move this around your room over a day. View the paint throughout different times of the day to ensure you love it consistently. You're then ready to get painting!

TA DAH! YOU HAVE SUCCESSFULLY SELECTED THE IDEAL WHITE FOR YOUR SPACE

Just remember, you may need more than one white for your house as your rooms are likely to face at least two different directions. So, if you want to achieve a 'neutral' white across the board, you will need to tailor the white for the room. For example, a warmer one for rooms at the front of your house that face north-east, a slightly cooler one for the rooms at the back of your house that receive south-west light.

I'm sure some people think I'm deranged because of the amount of time and energy I dedicate to discussing white paint, but it really can make or break a room. The perfect white is one that seamlessly joins your other colours, complementing and showcasing them to their full potential. And when you've gone to the effort of carefully curating your dream colour palette, you don't want to fall at the last sneaky ivory-tinted hurdle, do you?

07

THE
TECHNICAL
BITS

'If you love something, it will work. That's the only real rule.' **Bunny Williams, interior designer**

There are no real rules when it comes to interiors. Yes, you can employ useful tips and tricks to make the most of your space and colours, but these are just guidelines, which you may or may not choose to heed (although you have picked this book up – a good indication you're not a total maverick). It may not seem it at times but interior design is supposed to be fun, whimsical and a little frivolous. I'm not interested in gatekeeping treasured secrets – this isn't interior design MI5. **We all deserve a home that makes us feel content and welcomed every day**.

To confess, I am completely self-taught when it comes to colour, but when enough people come to you for guidance, it makes you step back and re-evaluate. Perhaps this isn't just an obsession with colour; maybe I do know what I'm talking about? Similar to when Harry realizes he actually *is* a wizard – a surreal and heartening moment, just on an ever-so-slightly smaller scale.

In this chapter, we'll cover the bits that can make or break a room. Our homes can go from bland to breathtaking with the sweep of a paintbrush, but the devil is always in the detail. The delicate dance between colours in a space, the vital importance of light (both natural and artificial), and how finishing touches can elevate the final result like icing on an already delicious cake.

COLOUR RATIOS

'I never met a colour
I didn't like.' **Dale Chihuly,
glass artist**

The term 'colour ratios' sounds extremely technical, when in reality it simply means the balance of quantities of colour within a room. One of the biggest concerns that always seems to rear its monochromatic head when creating a colour-filled home is the worry of it looking too busy, or 'a bit much'.

You want your space to be a warm welcome from your most-loved hues, but not necessarily a tirade of colour the moment you walk in the door. Some people are under the impression that a colourful home translates into over-stimulating chaos, but I can personally vouch that this is in no way the case.

Colour doesn't have to be daunting; you don't have to play it safe and settle for something that doesn't make you happy. It's just a case of keeping an eye on your palette's proportions to create that wonderfully balanced feel.

TOP TIPS FOR COLOUR RATIOS

70%, 20%, 10% & A DASH

This sounds worryingly close to maths, and dreaded percentages, but I promise it's not that serious or perplexing. These are just the rough quantities I note in my head when putting together a colour scheme. You start with your hero colour – let's go with mauve-pink. I know I want the room to feel mainly pink, so I'll use this on the walls, the curtains, some accessories and perhaps a large piece of furniture such as the sofa. **There is my 70%**. Next, I'll take my beta colour – one I've specifically chosen to complement the main colour, and add real pizzazz; for this scheme, it's honey yellow. I'll use this on a large piece of furniture,

like another sofa, and just one or two smaller pieces, such as a lampshade or cushion. **There is my 20%. Now for my 10%**, I usually go with something unexpected. I like a room to feel not too put together, so I'll throw in a sky blue – not a combination you see all the time, but I love it, so in it goes – in the form of very small touches: a cushion, and in this instance (see page 122), a log-burning fire. **Now all that's left are your dashes** – the other colours from around your home, so in my case green, plus the 70%, 20% and 10% colours. Your dash colours are your artwork, the myriad of hues in your rug – the tiny finishing sprinkles of colour magic. And there you have it – a colourful yet balanced room, in this case, our living room. Never chaotic, yet never dull either.

COMPLEMENT, THEN CONTRAST

As you would any great masterpiece, you want your rooms to lure people in, spark interest, and entice them to spend moments drinking in their wonder. The greatest rooms invite your eyes to roam. Try to provide a combination of **blissful complementary tones** that soothe, and **contrasts that draw the eye** around the space. Once you have selected your dominant colour, choose a secondary colour that harmonizes with it, and a third that provides an interesting contrast, enhancing all the hues.

COLOUR THERAPY

Colour is joy, optimism, nostalgia, intrigue and delight. The most important thing about any colour scheme is that it makes *you* happy. Life can sometimes be grim and weary, so filling your home with your most beloved colours will ensure you always have a place where you can take comfort and shelter from the storms of everyday existence. Forget trends, forget what your friends have gone for, forget what social media tells you your home needs to resemble; simply weave the colours you love into the fabric of your rooms, and you'll create a space you'll always be happy to come home to. As my favourite photographer Tim Walker once said, 'Just keep things simple, don't let technicality prevent you from expressing yourself.'

LIGHT DIRECTION

'Colours are the deeds of light.' **Johann Wolfgang von Goethe, writer**

Observing how the light of a single day alters colour is mesmerizing. Anyone who has sat curled up in a chair with a good book while the shadows of the day creep leisurely across the room will know the magic I'm referring to; from sunlit and glow-filled, to atmospheric and moody within a few hours, all from a shift in light. And I can guarantee that if you have experienced this, the room in which you did so was <u>not</u> north facing, or vice versa for southern hemisphere. No, I'm not Mystic Meg; that's just how light works. From season to season, hour to hour, or even room to room, our perception of a colour ebbs and flows with the ever-shifting natural light. Light is the reason you can't take a paint shade you have spotted in your friend's kitchen, paint it on your own walls and expect the same results. Without a doubt, the most common colour query I hear is 'I tried a paint sample that I saw in someone's house in a magazine, but it looks different in my house'. That is because, unfortunately, unless you actually *live* in their house, it won't. Your rooms aren't their rooms, and your light isn't their light. Let's not forget, <u>light is how we are able to perceive colour</u>; it is the *most* important element when choosing paint. Light should be at the top of the list when making any colour decision. Instead of trying to emulate a look, find a shade that's similar and, most importantly, tailored perfectly for the light in your own home.

TOP TIPS FOR LIGHT DIRECTION

EVERY ROOM COUNTS

Unless you're lucky enough to be a resident of The Shire and live in a hobbit house, with windows only on one side, you're going to have at least two different directions of light to deal with in your home. In order to make your life easy when choosing paint, you need to know which direction each room faces. Stand in your rooms facing the window with your compass (most smartphones have one) and make a note of the direction. It may be in between, for example north-east, so be sure to note this down.

KNOW YOUR LIGHTS

Now you have your light direction, what next? To try to make this as easy as possible to digest, I've listed the perceived pros and cons of each type of light. Once you grasp these, you will never pick the wrong paint again!

NORTH FACING

Pros: This is the light preferred by artists because of its steady and unchanging temperament, and lack of strong harsh shadows. North-facing light is reflected light; if you live in the northern hemisphere, the sun shines from the south, which means any north-facing spaces don't receive direct sunlight. North-facing light reflects off the sky, which is why it is cooler in nature. Because the light isn't shining directly from the sun into your windows, your room will stay cooler too! Okay, end of science lesson.

Cons: As north-facing light reflects from the sky, it has a cool blue cast to it. As a result your room will always feel on the fresher side, especially if you choose colours with blue, green, purple or grey undertones, as the northern light will greatly enhance their frosty appearance.

SOUTH FACING

Pros: South-facing light is the directional equivalent of a golden child. It sort of does no wrong. Warm and bright, it will bathe your rooms in beautiful light from morning to evening, and even the steeliest of hues will still manage to look pleasant in radiant yellow-toned southern light.

Cons: The only potential downside to a south-facing space is that because the light is direct and so much warmer than north facing, if you're someone who loves their colours cold and fresh, you will need to go *even* cooler to ensure the blue tones aren't cancelled out by the yellow light. Also, as the light travels across the room throughout the day, you will experience shadows aplenty. This is not normally an issue, unless you're an artist, in which case you may wish to execute your landscape painting elsewhere.

EAST & WEST FACING

Pros: With east- and west-facing rooms, you're blessed with almost a mix of both formerly mentioned lights. As the sun rises in the east, an east-facing space will be bathed in a golden glow in the morning; on the other hand, a west-facing room will receive the sun's last gleaming rays at the end of the day. While the sun isn't on your room, the space will take on the appearance of a cool north-facing one.

Cons: Due to the mercurial nature of light in east- and west-facing rooms, you need to consider two things – <u>when</u> you are going to be using the room most, and <u>what</u> colour works for both lights. For example, if your kitchen is east facing, you know that in the mornings while you enjoy breakfast you will be able to bask in beautiful direct sunlight. However, by the time you're making your evening meal, the light will have moved on and your room will feel much crisper. If you want your room to feel cosy even at the darker time of the day, pick a colour with rich yellow or brown undertones to cling on to that toasty feeling all day long.

WORK WITH WHAT YOU HAVE

You've taken note of the light directions, and you understand the perceived pros and cons of the light being delivered – however, you've hit a snag. You *really* had your heart set on a balmy, Mediterranean aesthetic for your living room, <u>but</u> you've just discovered it receives colder, north-facing light – now what?

Whatever directions your rooms face, it is a case of deciding whether you want to **embrace it, or counteract it** – depending on how *you* want the space to look and feel.

If the light is cooler, but you crave the warmth, go for colours with vigorous yellow undertones – perhaps stronger than you would have initially chosen – to ramp up the heat. The top yellow notes will be cancelled out by the blue north-facing light, but not all of them – meaning you'll still be left with plenty of warmth. On the contrary, if you *love* a modern and airy-feeling space, lean into the north-facing light with grey and blue undertones, and your room will feel exceptionally cool, always. Play about with your samples until you achieve the perfect equilibrium between light and colour.

USING ACCESSORIES

'Too much good taste can be very boring. Independent style on the other hand, can be very inspiring.' **Diana Vreeland, fashion editor**

I've always had an obsession with museums. Perhaps it's because of the abundance of history hidden behind their walls, or maybe it's just the curious (nosy) magpie in me, as I love to look at wonderful *things*. Give me a wee wonky handmade vase, or a chipped Victorian candlestick, and I'm in absolute heaven. Wandering the hushed halls of a museum, I'm in total awe of how many myths and tales each object holds about the people who once owned them. If only they could speak. This feeling is *precisely* what I love about the accessories within some peoples' homes.

Unexpected, individual, full of humour or charming character. You can walk in and instantly learn something more about the inhabitants. The items may be *completely* at odds with your own taste, and sometimes even a little peculiar, but that makes them all the more fascinating. We are all different, which is why it never works to fully emulate someone else's home; it's a carbon copy of a space that holds no meaning for you. Instead, be inspired, but put your own twist on the narrative – **use the items you love to fill your home with personality**. It doesn't matter whether you're a die-hard minimalist or a flamboyant uber-maximalist, the right accessories are the perfect way to bring individual identity to your home.

TOP TIPS FOR ACCESSORIES

STYLE & SUBSTANCE

Designer William Morris once professed, 'Have nothing in your houses that you do not know to be useful, or believe to be beautiful', and I truly think that mantra is what you should strive for when curating your home. All of us want our houses to be perceived as handsome and interesting, but if you buy things only when they become trendy, you will soon tire of them when they're subsequently washed out of fashion, on the tide of the latest 'in' thing. I would say I'm more a maximalist as I love things, *however* I don't just like having things for the sake of it.

Yes, I have a fair few vases, a plethora of plates, and enough candlestick holders to host an impromptu séance (you just <u>never</u> know), but all these things have a use and purpose too – in addition to being beautiful! When cupboard space is at a premium, which is in most houses, if you have items that are pretty as well as practical – like a water jug that lives a double life as a vase, or a plate that can transform into a table centrepiece – you will save on space, *plus* have the enjoyment of using beautiful things every day for even the most mundane of tasks. It really does lift your mood. Go eat your next meal off a charming, special plate and tell me this isn't the case.

QUALITY OVER QUANTITY

When it comes to furnishing or accessorizing rooms, the money can quickly begin to rack up – especially if it's a whole house you're trying to fill. New quality furniture is very appealing, but the price – not so much. Luckily for us, there is a much more budget-friendly way of acquiring decent furniture and the finishing touches for your home: buying secondhand. The people who know me are now wondering how I've managed to hold off until *this* late in the book to mention this. There is a world of the loveliest quality furniture out there, be it from charity shops, eBay, antique fairs, Facebook Marketplace, car-boot sales, local swap sites – the list is pretty endless. These pieces may have lived a life or two previously, and some things may need a clean down or a lick of paint, but these are items built to last – because that's *precisely* what they have

done. You will never regret buying a secondhand piece of furniture – you always have the satisfaction of knowing that if you had purchased it brand new, it would likely have cost five times the price, if not more. You are also ensuring your home has a unique edge – it's unlikely you'll meet someone else with the exact desk or vintage lamp very regularly. Even if money was no object, I would still encourage people to buy secondhand. The items in our home that receive the most love and attention from guests are always the ones I picked up for a couple of quid from a charity shop, or some absolute unicorn of an antique that I found on Marketplace. Great quality, unique, excellent value, fantastic for the environment... the list of positives goes on. You might not be able to browse online, but I promise you, once you start shopping secondhand, you won't be able to stop. *Climbs down from soapbox.*

SCALE & PROPORTIONS

You may view your house as averaged sized, but that doesn't mean you have to play it safe when it comes to choosing pieces for your rooms. Unexpected contrasts between oversized, larger objects and diminutive little items keep a space interesting. The substantial size of one thing serves to enhance and highlight the delicate nature of another. An enormous ginger jar table lamp taking centre stage beside a dinky arm chair, or two tiny symmetrical wall lights either side of a vast ornate emperor bed – the unexpected scale adds a sublime element of contrast in the room, and we all know how contrasts serve to bring out the best in situations. They aren't in competition with one another; in fact, their differences highlight just how wonderful each of them is! More bang for your buck, so to speak.

ARTIFICIAL LIGHTING

'Lighting is everything. It creates atmosphere, drama and intrigue in a room.'
Martyn Lawrence Bullard, interior designer

If I had a pound for every time I'd told someone, 'what you need is a lamp, or three', I'd probably be able to start my own international lighting empire, ensuring that every home is properly lit. Perhaps I'll save this venture for my retirement. Just as natural light is fundamental to how a colour appears on your walls, **artificial lighting has its own integral part to play** in creating the *feel* and atmosphere you want to achieve in your home. As my amazing grandma Sylvia says: 'It's all about the ambience darling!'. And she is <u>100% correct</u>. This is the woman who, for as long as I've been alive, has had no lightbulbs in any of her ceiling pendants, just in case anyone tries (dares) to turn on the overhead light – mistakenly or otherwise. This is why galleries mount ornate brass wall lights over historic works of art, and why you adore your favourite Italian restaurant with its secluded corners of amber glow. Great lighting is the difference between walking in and feeling welcomed – wanting to linger, relax and unwind – versus wincing in a stark bright space with zero intrigue, mystery or warmth, eager to grab your coat and leave. That, my friends, is the power of the lamp. No genie required.

TOP TIPS FOR ARTIFICIAL LIGHT

CONTRASTS ARE KEY

Artificial lighting is *sort* of comparable to being best friends with Dr Jekyll. Use it well and it works seamlessly to make the most of *every* room, ensuring your home *feels precisely* the way you always dreamed it would. Use it incorrectly, and Mr Hyde will scare away your guests, and leave you on edge as soon as the dark creeps in. Your artificial lighting should enhance your space, drawing eyes around the room to enhance the details and create cosy corners. Darker areas add interest – again, contrasts are key when it comes to interiors – so use lamps dotted around to create pools of light and areas of shadow. If you only use an overhead light, this will flatten your space, as it will completely flood all areas with a bright (and extremely unflattering) light at once – no intrigue, no warm ambient glow; it'll feel like a petrol-station forecourt, definitely not somewhere you or your guests will want to linger.

LOW FOR GLOW

In an ideal situation, your lighting should be average-head height or lower to create a proper ambient glow. Overhead lighting – such as spotlights, or 'the big light' – are great for creating clean lines (and making it bright enough to perform minor surgery in your front room), but are incredibly unflattering, casting deep shadows on you and your furniture, and highlighting any imperfections.

When you're on holiday, do you take your most flattering pictures at midday with the sun beating down directly overhead? No, of course not; you take them just before sunset at golden hour, when the rosy light is warm and facing you at low level. All you need to do now apply this principle to your home. Even a super-slick, modern or industrial home will benefit from ambient lighting. Lamps are the ultimate tools for highlighting a room's details and best features, so use them to your advantage.

MULTIPLE SOURCES

Now when I tell you that you could do with having at least three lamps per room, you might think I've completely lost it. I know it sounds slightly excessive, but in an average-sized room, there is more than adequate space! Think of lighting your room like constructing a harmonious symphony: a drop of light, a dash of dark – the fluctuation of bright to shadows is a delicious contrast. If you just stuck with the one lamp, the rest of your room would be shrouded in darkness, giving the impression of a solitary lighthouse in a storm. Not exactly cosy. Start with the first lamp, then consider where else in your space you want to highlight. Once those two lamps are in situ, it will become obvious where the last area of glow needs to go. For added interest, use a mixture of table lamps, standing lamps and even wall lights – the world of ambient lighting is a truly beautiful one.

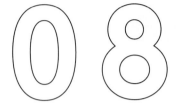

PAINT

'Interiors speak. Rooms emphasize whether one simply exists or lives, and there is a great difference between the two.' **Van Day Truex, interior designer**

Paint – magic in liquid form and the ultimate tool in decorating. Nothing transforms a space like the ideal colours, and there is no easier or more cost-effective way of incorporating these colours than by going to town on your walls with a paintbrush. Yes, colourful furnishings and paraphernalia can elevate interiors, but when you add the *perfect* colour to the walls, the space really does *sing*.

You now have your paint colours nailed down, your palette selected and your moodboard – a veritable work of art – ready. All that's left is to **pick your paint**. But wait... what on earth are all these different options? If you don't understand paint varieties, I can relate. I have the same fear when I'm sent to the bar to place everyone's wine order. Because I don't drink, I'm completely clueless. I'm about to ask for 'four white wines, please' when I spot a menu with 27 options hanging above the spirit bottles and not *one* of them says just 'white wine'. Fantastic. I guess it'll have to be wine Russian roulette for my friends' drinks. But you don't have to suffer the same fate. I'm here to provide you with what is effectively a paint menu: a breakdown of the different types of paint, and where you can use them. **Your dream room is only a tin of paint away!**

VARIETIES & FINISHES OF PAINT

FOR YOUR WALLS & CEILINGS

Emulsion is probably the best-known type of paint – suitable for your interior walls and ceilings and available in matt and silk:

MATT

- Depending on the paint brand, matt paint may be prefixed by terms such as 'pure', 'flat', 'estate', 'absolute', 'modern', 'architect', 'marble', and so on. Don't let this bamboozle you. If you're not sure, matt emulsion is usually the top swatch on any example page of your colour card, and the one with the least shine.

- Matt paint has anywhere from a 2% to 7% sheen level – the lower the sheen, the truer the colour payoff, as it reflects less light. Stately homes and art galleries opt for a flat matt finish to achieve a rich and luxurious depth of colour. Another positive is that the flat and light-diffusing nature of matt paint makes it fantastic for disguising bumps and imperfections on your walls!

- It is often stated that the low sheen of matt paints means they are less likely to withstand a full scrubbing, should they need it. That said, our walls are painted exclusively in matt paint and I've never had an issue cleaning them – this will depend entirely on what you're wiping off your walls, and how regularly you're doing it, so be sure to consider this if cleaning the walls is high on your priority list.

SILK

- This semi-sheen paint is a step up from matt when it comes to shine. With a sheen level of anything from 20% to 40%, silk paint bounces an abundance of light around the space, so it's ideal if you have somewhere dark to decorate.

- Silk paint's shiny and reflective nature means the colour payoff isn't as intense as with matt paint. Nor is it *hugely* flattering on bumpy plaster or textured surfaces, so you could find yourself noticing imperfections on your walls if you opt for silk.

- More shine means that silk paint is fully washable – ideal if you or the other inhabitants of the house love to rub their hands, or paws, all over the walls...

FOR YOUR WOOD & METAL

These paints can be used on anything from internal doors and architraves, to skirting boards, floorboards and for upcycling furniture.

EGGSHELL

- This paint is exactly what it sounds like: once dried, it resembles the texture of an eggshell – almost matt but with an *ever-so-slight* hint of soft shine.

- Eggshell is the closest equivalent to a matt finish in a wood- and metal-friendly paint, so if all your walls are painted in matt and you want your skirting boards and doors to have a comparable finish, eggshell is for you.

- As with all paint formulated for wood and metal surfaces, eggshell is extremely durable – making it ideal for high traffic areas such as your kitchen cupboards.

SATIN

- The wood and metal equivalent of silk emulsion, AKA the middle child. Not as flat and subdued as eggshell, yet not as shiny and eye catching as gloss.

- Just as eggshell ties in flawlessly with matt, satin is the ultimate companion for luminous silk-coated walls. Just be wary of any uneven surfaces, as it has the same tendency to make any imperfections more pronounced.

- Satin's increased level of shine and durability means it is often the decorator's paint of choice for bathrooms and kitchens, as it resists moisture very effectively.

GLOSS

- Bright, shiny and lustrous. Most of us probably grew up in houses with white-gloss skirting boards and doors. Its extremely shiny and wipeable finish made it a popular choice for items that needed to be wiped down often, as the dust just slides straight off its gleaming surface.

- Gloss paint used to be oil based, which meant it was *exceptionally* shiny – but also meant it took a full 24 hours to dry, had an extremely pungent smell (all those dangerous Volatile Organic Compounds, or VOCs – paint is now advertised as low or zero VOC) and involved you getting the white spirits out to clean your brushes. These days you'd struggle to find an oil-based paint in some stores most online retailers now only sell water-based paint, even gloss! You can still achieve a 95% shine level with a water-based gloss finish, so everyone's a winner really – our lungs included.

- Although definitely not the most sympathetic paint to uneven surfaces, gloss is great for adding drama or highlighting a focal area – a beautiful ornate banister or staircase looks even more impressive in a glossy finish.

CHALK

- A relatively new paint on the block, chalk finish paint was originally invented by Annie Sloane with the specific objective of upcycling furniture. Many alternative brands have since sprung up in a medley of colours.

- Chalk has a completely dead-flat finish, which is ideal for lending a vintage feel to old furniture. However, as it's designed for wood and metal, there is nothing stopping you from using it on your doors and other woodwork.

- Unlike other wood-friendly paints, chalk paint requires no prep (I know, seems odd) as long as the surface is clean and dry. Personally I would always give a very gentle sand to bare wood, so as to ensure a *perfect* grip on the paint, but that's me. If you want to add some extra durability at the end, apply a clear wax or varnish to seal in your hard work, and help avoid chips and scuffs. Unless you like that worn look!

TIPS FOR YOUR PAINTING PROJECTS

PREP, PREP & YES, YOU GUESSED IT, MORE PREP

I know it's loathsome and tedious – I know that sometimes you'd rather poke your own eye out with a paintbrush than get the sandpaper out – but it has to be done. Before you crack on with painting, ensure you've completed all the filling and sanding you need to get that faultless finish. Stick on a podcast or some music, and work away at all those imperfections and holes in your walls and woodwork. If not, you'll only fixate on them once you're finished and wish you'd done the proper prep work beforehand. Don't say I didn't warn you.

CHOOSING THE RIGHT PAINTING IMPLEMENT FOR THE JOB WILL MAKE YOUR LIFE SO MUCH EASIER

For cutting in, select a small angled brush with firm bristles to get that clean, sharp edge; for painting a larger piece of furniture, such as a sideboard or wardrobe, opt for a small foam roller rather than a brush – it will give a lovely smooth finish, and also save your arm falling off as it makes the job quicker. For ceilings, try using a paint pad – unlike a roller, it creates zero splash back and the coverage in one swipe is truly incredible.

IF POSSIBLE, TRY TO COMPLETE YOUR PAINTING IN DAYLIGHT

I know it's sometimes tempting to keep going through the evening to get the job finished but from experience I always find I end up missing areas, and have to go over them again when I come to inspect your handiwork in the morning. Better to split the work over two days and achieve your perfect room than rush to complete everything in one day and get a patchy finish. We're striving for flawless, not fast.

A FINAL WORD

'It's not what you look at that matters, it's what you see.' **Henry David Thoreau**

If you had told me five, no even three years ago, that I would have the opportunity to write a book, all about helping people embrace more colour in their homes, I definitely would have laughed – and then once I realized you weren't joking, given you a look of deep concern. The truth is, even though I am ridiculously passionate about colour, I was never too sure where this road was heading, if anywhere. I am a person who loves to love things; it's always the best piece of cake, the most resplendent view, the greatest cloudscape; people may laugh, but why not? Why shouldn't you really love things. And that's exactly what happened with colour. I fell for it, embraced it like an old friend and never let it go. From dressing in full colour to hunting down every colourful door or building I could discover, I was hooked. But even in my wildest dreams, I didn't anticipate that creating The House That Colour Built, and sharing images of our home on Instagram, would lead to becoming part of a glorious community – one who also wanted to embrace a more colour-packed way of life. As I mentioned in the intro to this book, it really isn't about rainbow walls and psychedelic curtains (unless that's what you love) – I want people to discover their own unique version of colourful, and make their home a personal haven. And if this book successfully helps you to do so, then my work here is done.

THANKS

There are so many incredible people who have supported me with this book.

My first thank you goes out to Harriet Butt, my editor, for being the person who opened up the phenomenal world of writing to me properly, and helped me realize where my passion for colour was headed all along.

To Emily Lapworth, designer extraordinaire: thank you for bringing my colourful visions to life better than I even imagined – you are a wizard.

Also, a huge thank you to Anna, Chloe and Milly, who along with Harriet and Emily made the photoshoot for the book the most enjoyable experience ever – the house has never been so tidy and so messy simultaneously.

Thank you to my marvellous and insane family: my amazing mum, dad, sister JENNA (see Jenna, told you I'd get you in there, I even made your name capitalized), my gran (from whom I inherited any interior skills), auntie, and all my spectacular Sowerby-side, who, bizarrely, never doubted me or my ability to write for *one* second, even when I most definitely did.

My beloved friends, the ultimate cheerleaders, who checked in with me constantly to ensure I wasn't cracking under the pressure, provided a fantastic sounding board, and encouraged me to reward myself with more chocolate (joke's on them, I need no encouragement). To Merla, our wonderful dog who was my office companion the entire time I was writing this book – she never said much but she always heard me out.

And of course, Rick, my remarkable husband – quite literally the best human to ever exist. His unwavering faith in me is rather astonishing; if anyone can make you feel like *anything is possible*, it's this man.

I know I'm in danger of this tipping over into Oscar-acceptance-speech length, so one final thank you – to you. Each and every one of you who believed in me, supported me and cheered me on – it has made my colour-filled dream come true, more than you will ever know.

ABOUT THE AUTHOR

After buying her first house in 2019 with husband Rick and dog Merla, Rochdale-born Jessica Sowerby realized her lifelong passion for colour had finally found its perfect playground. While undertaking the home renovation, and setting up her Instagram @thehousethatcolourbuilt to document progress, Jessica gained an incredible community of like-minded followers. Featured in publications such as *The Sunday Times*, *The Guardian* and *Stylist* magazine, the Instagram platform allowed Jessica to share her knowledge of colourful interiors, and establish her own colour consultancy business – now helping a worldwide client base bring joy their homes. Jessica believes that **colour actually improves your life**, a house should always have a chocolate cupboard, and that dogs are better than most humans.

Colour Confidence is Jessica's first book – for more colourful inspiration, visit @thehousethatcolourbuilt

CREDITS

We have made every effort to contact and credit all the makers, artists and designers whose work appears incidentally in the book and will be more than happy to correct listings or add any omissions in future reprints.

LIVING ROOM

Artwork by K. Williams and Michael Donne; Other artwork from antique shops, Wallflower Vintage Art Gallery, Pathos Studio UK; Circle cushion from Lumikello Studio; Cushions from TK Maxx, Ikea, H&M, and eBay, Kip and Co; Lamp and Lampshade from Pooky; Sofas from Swoon; Rug from Rug Vista; Vase from Anthropologie.

BACK ROOM

Print 'James Spencer with Unicorn in Casket' by Tim Walker; Print by Margaret Jeane; Wrapping paper from Cavallini Papers; Rug from Rug Vista; Plant pot from TK Maxx; Light from lights.com; Sofa from AMC, Lamp from TK Maxx; Lampshade from Pooky; Blanket from John Lewis; Cushion from Katy Takla.

UTILITY

Lampshade from eBay; Small lampshade from Pooky; Bowl from Homesense; Wallpaper from Walpaper Direct.

KITCHEN

Pot by Proudly Potty; Candlesticks from Habit Haus; Blind by So Jorgeous; Vases from Oliver Bonas; Tablecloth and lamp from eBay; Lampshade painted by the author.

HALLWAY

LED neon sign by Yellowpop; Wrapping paper from Cavallini Papers; Other prints from Silver Lining Art Studio and Pink Polar Bear; Light from Pooky, Plant pot from Homesense.

BEDROOM

Cushion from Poppy and Honesty; Pillow case from Kip and Co.

OFFICE

Artwork by S. Durrans; Other artwork from Wallflower Vintage Art Gallery; Cloud plate from Urban Outfitters; Lamp from Homesense; Plantpots painted by the author and from Sainsbury's; Mugs from TK Maxx; Blind by So Jorgeous.

Managing Director Sarah Lavelle
Senior Commissioning Editor Harriet Butt
Senior Designer Emily Lapworth
Photographer Anna Batchelor
Stylist Milly Bruce
Head of Production Stephen Lang
Senior Production Controller
Sabeena Atchia

Published in 2023 by Quadrille,
an imprint of Hardie Grant Publishing

Quadrille
52–54 Southwark Street
London SE1 1UN
quadrille.com

Cataloguing in Publication Data:
a catalogue record for this book is
available from the British Library

Reprinted in 2024
10 9 8 7 6 5 4 3 2

ISBN 978 1 83783 028 2

Printed in China using soy inks